Waking From Dreams

Also by Judith E.P. Johnson

Mountain Moods (VDL Publications, 1997)
Gatherers (VDL Publications, 1998)
Fragments (VDL Publications, 2000)
Selected Poems CD (7 RPH, 2001)
Snapshot (Regal Press, 2003)
Landmarks (Ginninderra Press, 2005)
Alone at the Window (Ginninderra Press, 2012)
Between Two Moons (Ginninderra Press, 2015)

Judith E.P. Johnson

Waking from Dreams
haiku & senryu

Acknowledgements

Special thanks are due again to Peter Macrow for his kindness and inspiration; to my children Karen, Debra, and Craig for their support and encouragement; to Lyn Reeves for editing this book; and to Ron Moss for the art and design of the cover.

The author's haiku and senryu have been published in *Famous Reporter*, *Tasmanian Times*, *poam*, *paper wasp*, *Blue Giraffe*, *Shamrock*, *Haiku Oz*, *Prospect*, *Still Heading Out*, *Poetry Matters*, *Poetic Reflections*, *Pause for Poetry* and *Kō*.

Waking from Dreams: haiku & senryu
ISBN 978 1 76041 198 5
Copyright © text Judith E.P. Johnson 2016

First published 2016 by
Ginninderra Press
PO Box 3461 Port Adelaide SA 5015
www.ginninderrapress.com.au

for Graeme

coming out of the mountains
how high the moon
over the valley

river roadside
we wait
while ducks take their time

silence
after clear-felling –
a wild violet

dark shed
the pale faces
of unpainted gnomes

sweeping out the shed
rattle
of snail shells

overgrown lawn
up to my ankles
in daisies

high-rise car park
the sudden echo
of children's laughter

one hundred brushstrokes
for granddaughter's hair
spring sunshine

new leaves
schoolchildren
fold origami birds

rain puddle
a jasmine flower drifts
to its reflection

moon viewing
from the swamp
a chorus of frogs

your death day
I receive a posy
fragrant with rosemary

so far away
full moon at your window
and mine

Blackbird

midday sun
blackbird bathes
in the dog's drinking bowl

leafy hedge
beak full of grass
the blackbird disappears

on the lawn
a blackbird listens
for worms

jasmine bush
in out and in again
the blackbird

dawn
again over the treetops
blackbird singing

daybreak
at the dog beach
the growling surf

sea fog
even the mountain
has gone

cloudless sky
a pelican flies low
over clear blue waters

running along the beach the wind and I

cloud shadows
across the dunes
the echo of waves

soft sand
we follow the footprints
of a seagull

after last night's rain
wisteria and jasmine
reach for each other

heatwave
a hot shower
from the garden hose

warm breeze
moving the garden seat
for the beehive

new hive
a bee chases the dog
across the lawn

honeysuckle
all over the fence
bees

clear water
pond weeds shiver
in sunlight

decorated cake
I move wise men
for a slice

smelling the roses
a flurry of petals
round the old couple

twilight
a silent breeze
through the wind chime

drinking champagne
the stars in her eyes

late homecoming
softly I tread
the path of moonshine

along lover's lane
you and I
and the moon

how high the bright moon
shining in the river

juniper oil
forests of Latvia
scent my bathwater

while I sleep
under the stars
moon flowers open

after the day's heat
the still moon

King Island

Roaring Forties
a shipwreck plaque
on a mass grave

flickering
around the Calcified Forest
leaf shadows

handcrafted magnets
kelp hats, kelp boots,
kelp seahorses

late afternoon
cows follow the milk road
home

sunset
at Wickham Lighthouse
the longest shadow

another celebration
again I wear
great-grandmother's ring

falling leaves
a bird's nest appears
against the sky

high winds in conifers
all the pine cones
in the grass

after the bonfire
the bonfire
in my clothes

bonfire embers
a flame-robin
moves closer

in patchwork farmland
remnants
of the bush

tour guide
at a convict graveside
retold story retold

friends' get-together
grandmothers quoting
grandchildren

china teacups
from the mirrored cabinet
my face looks out

slide montage
at the anniversary concert
you join us

misty moonlight
even the river gums
are ghosts

city lights
how noisy
under the silent moon

awake at 2 a.m.
all those voices
on my radio

dawn
another day
across your grave

leaves spinning back to earth April rain

Flinders Island

in still blue waters
all that remains
of a shipwreck

puffs of foam
blowing along the sand
bubble shells

clouds cover the sun
darkness in the church
at Wybalenna

trembling in the wind
wild flowers
on an unmarked grave

silver jewel box
maireener shell necklace
on black velvet

morning frost
ice ferns
melt on my window

this chilly day
the caged radiance
of your fire

laid out
in the old tin trunk
wide-eyed dolls

all those years gone
in one puff
eightieth birthday

grey sky
through frosted park trees
distant church bells

loud
in the chattering crowd
my silent thoughts

here I am
at your graveside
where are you?

bitter wind
how lonely your name
in the crowded cemetery

a long time on your grave dead flowers

leaving your grave
how long the road
into winter

waking from dreams full moon

www.ingramcontent.com/pod-product-compliance
Lightning Source LLC
Chambersburg PA
CBHW062206100526
44589CB00014B/1983